LUCY
I am afraid you are angry with me, Papa.

GOODWILL
Be not frighten'd, my dear Child, you have done nothing to offend me. But answer me one Question—What does my little Dear think of a Husband?

LUCY
A Husband, Papa! Ola!

GOODWILL
Come, it is a Question a Girl in her Sixteenth Year may answer. Shou'd you like to have a Husband, Lucy?

LUCY
And am I to have a Coach?

GOODWILL
No, no: What has that to do with a Husband?

LUCY
Why you know, Papa, Sir John Wealthy's Daughter was carry'd away in a Coach by her Husband; and I have been told by several of our Neighbours, that I was to have a Coach when I was marry'd. Indeed, I have dreamt of it a hundred hundred times. I never dreamt of a Husband in my whole Life, that I did not dream of a Coach. I have rid about in one all Night in my Sleep, and methought it was the purest thing!—

GOODWILL
Lock up a Girl as you will, I find, you cannot keep her from evil Counsellors.
[Aside]
I tell you, Child, you must have no Coach with a Husband.

LUCY
Then let me have one without a Husband.

GOODWILL
What, had you rather have a Coach than a Husband?

LUCY
Hum—I don't know that.—But, if you'll get me a Coach, let me alone, I'll warrant I'll get me a Husband.

AIR I
Thomas, I cannot.

Do you, Papa, but find a Coach,
And leave the other to me, Sir;
For that will make the Lover approach,
And I warrant we shan't disagree, Sir.
No Sparks will talk

To Girls that walk,
I've heard it, and I confide in't:
Do you then fix
My Coach and Six,
I warrant I get one to ride in't, to ride in't,
I warrant, &c.

GOODWILL

The Girl is out of her Wits, sure. Hussy! who put these Thoughts into your Head? You shall have a good sober Husband, that will teach you better things.

LUCY

Ay, but I won't tho', if I can help it; for Miss Jenny Flant-it says, a sober Husband is the worst sort of Husband in the World.

GOODWILL

I have a Mind to sound the Girl's Inclinations. Come hither, Lucy; tell me now, of all the Men you ever saw, whom shou'd you like best for a Husband?

LUCY

O fy, Papa, I must not tell.

GOODWILL

Yes, you may your Father.

LUCY

No, Miss Jenny says I must not tell my Mind to any Man whatever. She never tells a Word of Truth to her Father.

GOODWILL

Miss Jenny is a wicked Girl, and you must not regard her. Come, tell me the Truth, or I shall be angry.

LUCY

Why then, of all the Men I ever saw in my whole Life-time, I like Mr. Thomas, my Lord Bounce's Footman the best, a hundred thousand times.

GOODWILL

Oh, fy upon you! like a Footman?

LUCY

A Footman! he looks a thousand times more like a Gentleman than either Squire Foxchase or Squire Tankard, and talks more like one, ay, and smells more like one too. His Head is so prettily drest, done all down upon the top with Sugar, like a frosted Cake, with three little Curls of each side, that you may see his Ears as plain! and then, his Hair is done up behind just like a fine Lady's, with a little little Hat, and a Pair of charming white Stockins, as neat and as fine as any white-legg'd Fowl; and he always carries a great swinging Stick in his Hand, as big as himself, that he wou'd knock any Dog down with who was to offer to bite me. A Footman indeed! why Miss Jenny likes him as well as I do, and she says all the fine young Gentlemen that the Ladies in London are so fond of, are just such Persons as he is.—Icod, I shou'd

An Old Man Taught Wisdom by Henry Fielding

or, THE VIRGIN UNMASK'D. A FARCE

As it is Perform'd By His MAJESTY's Company of Comedians at the Theatre-Royal in Drury-Lane.

Henry Fielding was born at Sharpham Park, near Glastonbury, in Somerset on April 22nd 1707. His early years were spent on his parents' farm in Dorset before being educated at Eton.

An early romance ended disastrously and with it his removal to London and the beginnings of a glittering literary career; he published his first play, at age 21, in 1728.

He was prolific, sometimes writing six plays a year, but he did like to poke fun at the authorities. His plays were thought to be the final straw for the authorities in their attempts to bring in a new law. In 1737 The Theatrical Licensing Act was passed. At a stroke political satire was almost impossible. Fielding was rendered mute. Any playwright who was viewed with suspicion by the Government now found an audience difficult to find and therefore Theatre owners now toed the Government line.

Fielding was practical with the circumstances and ironically stopped writing to once again take up his career in the practice of law and became a barrister after studying at Middle Temple. By this time he had married Charlotte Craddock, his first wife, and they would go on to have five children. Charlotte died in 1744 but was immortalised as the heroine in both Tom Jones and Amelia.

Fielding was put out by the success of Samuel Richardson's Pamela, or Virtue Rewarded. His reaction was to spur him into writing a novel. In 1741 his first novel was published; the successful Shamela, an anonymous parody of Richardson's novel.

Undoubtedly the masterpiece of Fielding's career was the novel Tom Jones, published in 1749. It is a wonderfully and carefully constructed picaresque novel following the convoluted and hilarious tale of how a foundling came into a fortune.

Fielding was a consistent anti-Jacobite and a keen supporter of the Church of England. This led to him now being richly rewarded with the position of London's Chief Magistrate. Fielding continued to write and his career both literary and professional continued to climb.

In 1749 he joined with his younger half-brother John, to help found what was the nascent forerunner to a London police force, the Bow Street Runners. Fielding's ardent commitment to the cause of justice in the 1750s unfortunately coincided with a rapid deterioration in his health. Such was his decline that in the summer of 1754 he travelled, with Mary and his daughter, to Portugal in search of a cure. Gout, asthma, dropsy and other afflictions forced him to use crutches. His health continued to fail alarmingly.

Henry Fielding died in Lisbon two months later on October 8th, 1754.

DRAMATIS PERSONÆ

Goodwill
Lucy, his Daughter
Blister, an Apothecary
Coupee, a Dancing-Master
Bookish, a Student
Quaver, a Singing-Master
Wormwood, a Lawyer
Mr. Thomas, a Footman

SCENE: A Hall in Goodwill's House in the Country.

AN OLD MAN TAUGHT WISDOM

GOODWILL [Solus]
Well! it is to me surprising, that out of the Multitudes who feel a Pleasure in getting an Estate, few or none shou'd taste a Satisfaction in bestowing it. Doubtless a good Man must have vast Delight in rewarding Merit, nor will I believe it so difficult to be found. I am at present, I thank Heav'n, and my own Industry, worth a good 10000 l. and an only Daughter; both which I have determin'd to give to the most worthy of my poor Relations. The Transport I feel from the Hope of making some honest Man happy, makes me amends for the many weary Days, and sleepless Nights my Riches have cost me. The Girl I have bred up under my own Eye; she has seen nothing, knows nothing, and has consequently no Will but mine. I have no Reason to doubt her Consent to whatever Choice I shall make.—How happily must my Old Age slide away, between the Affection of an innocent and dutiful Child, and the grateful Return I may expect from a so much obliged Son-in-law! I am certainly the happiest Man on Earth.

[Enter **LUCY**.

LUCY
Did you send for me, Papa?

GOODWILL
Yes, come hither, Child. I have sent for you to mention an Affair to you, which you, I believe, have not yet thought of

LUCY
I hope it is not to send me to a Boarding-School, Papa.

GOODWILL
I hope my Indulgence to you has been such, that you have Reason to regard me as the best of Fathers. I am sure I have never deny'd you any thing, but for your own Good: Indeed I have consulted nothing else. It is that for which I have been toiling these many Years; for which I have deny'd my self ev'ry Comfort in Life; and from which I have, from renting a Farm of 500 a Year, amassed the Sum of 10000l.

have had him before now, but that Folks told me I shou'd have a Man with a Coach, and that methinks I had rather have a great and a great deal.

GOODWILL
I am amaz'd! But I abhor the mercenary Temper in the Girl, worse than all.—What, Child, wou'd you have any one with a Coach? Wou'd you have Mr. Achum?

LUCY
Yes indeed, wou'd I, for a Coach.

GOODWILL
Why, he is a Cripple, and can scarce walk across the Room.

LUCY
What signifies that?

AIR II
Wully Honey.

When he in a Coach can be carry'd,
What need has a Man to go?
That Women for Coaches are marry'd,
I'm not such a Child but I know.
But if the poor crippled Elf
In Coach be not able to roam,
Why then I can go by my self,
And he may e'en stay at home.

[Enter **BLISTER**.

BLISTER
Mr. Goodwill, your humble Servant. I have rid twelve long Miles in little more than an Hour. I am glad to see you so well; I was afraid by your Message—

GOODWILL
That I had wanted your Advice, I suppose; but truly, Coz, I sent for you on a better Account.—Lucy, this is a Relation of yours, you have not seen a great while, my Cousin Blister, the Apothecary.

LUCY
O la! I hope that great huge Man is not to be my Husband.

BLISTER
My Cousin is well grown, and looks healthy. What Apothecary do you employ? He deals in good Drugs, I warrant him.

GOODWILL
Plain wholesome Food and Exercise are what she deals in.

BLISTER
Plain wholesome Food is very proper at some time of the Year, with gentle Physick between whiles.

GOODWILL
Leave us a little, my dear Lucy, I must talk with your Cousin.

LUCY
Yes, Papa, with all my Heart—I hope I shall never see that great Thing again.

[Exit.

GOODWILL
I believe you begin to wonder at my Message, and will perhaps more, when you know the Occasion of it. In short, without more Preface, I begin to find my self going out of the World, and my Daughter very eager to come into it. I have therefore resolv'd to see her settled without farther Delay. I am far from thinking vast Wealth necessary to Happiness: Wherefore, as'I can give her a sufficient Competency. I slave determined to marry her to one of my own Relations. It will please me, that the Fruits of my Labour shou'd not go out of the Family. I have sent to several of my Kinsmen, of whom she shall take her Choice; and as you are the first here, if you like my Proposal, you shall make the first Application.

BLISTER
With all my Heart, Cousin; and I am very much oblig'd to you. Your Daughter seems an agreeable young Woman, and I have no Aversion to Marriage. But pray, why do you think your self going out of the World? Proper Care might continue you in it a considerable while. Let me feel your Pulse.

GOODWILL
To oblige you; tho' I am in very good Health.

BLISTER
A little feverish.—I wou'd advise you to lose a little Blood, and take an Emulsion, with a gentle Emetick an Cathartick.

GOODWILL
No, no, I will send my Daughter to you; but pray keep your Physick to your self, dear Cousin.

[Exit.

BLISTER
This Man is near Seventy, and, I have heard, never took any Physick in his Life, and yet he looks as well as if he had been under the Doctor's Hands all his Life-time. 'Tis strange; but if I marry his Daughter, the sooner he dies, the better. It is an odd Whim of his to marry her in this manner; but he is very rich, and so, so much the better.—What a strange Dowdy 'tis! no Matter, her Fortune is never the worse.

AIR III
Round, round the Mill.

In Women we Beauty or Wit may admire;
Sing Trol, lerol.

But sure as we have them, as surely they'll tire;
Oh ho, will they so?
Abroad for these Dainties the Wise therefore roam,
Sing Trol lerol.
And frugally keep but a plain Dish at home;
Oh ho, do they so?
Who marries a Beauty, must hate her when old;
Sing Trol lerol.
But the older it grows, the more precious the Gold.
Oh ho, is it so?

[Enter **LUCY**.

Oh, here comes my Mistress: What a Pox shall I say to her? I never made Love in my Life.

LUCY
Papa has sent me hither; but if it was not for fear of a Boarding-School, I am sure I wou'd not have come; but they say I shall be whipt there, and a Husband can't whip me, let me do what I will; that's one good thing.

BLISTER
Won't you please to sit down, Cousin?

LUCY
Yes, thank you, Sir.—Since I must stay with you I may as well sit down as not.

BLISTER
Pray, Cousin, how do you find your self?

LUCY
Find my self?

BLISTER
Yes, how do you do? Let me feel your Pulse. How do you sleep o' Nights?

LUCY
How? why upon my back, generally.

BLISTER
But I mean, do you sleep without Interruption? are you not restless?

LUCY
I tumble and toss a good deal, sometimes.

BLISTER
Hum! Pray how long do you usually sleep?

LUCY

About ten or eleven Hours.

BLISTER
Is your Stomach good? Do you eat with an Appetite? How often do you find in a Day any Inclination to eat?

LUCY
Why, a good many times; but I don't eat a great deal, unless it be at Breakfast, Dinner, and Supper, and Afternoon's Nunchion.

BLISTER
Hum! I find you have at present no absolute need of an Apothecary.

LUCY
I am glad to hear that, I wish he was gone with all my Heart.

BLISTER
I suppose, Cousin, your Father has mentioned to you the Affair I am come upon; may I hope you will comply with him, in making me the happiest Man upon Earth?

LUCY
You need not ask me, you know I must do what he bids me.

BLISTER
May I then hope you will make me your Husband?

LUCY
I must do what he'll have me.

BLISTER
What makes you cry, Miss?
Pray tell me what is the matter.

LUCY
No, you will be angry with me, if I tell you.

BLISTER
I Angry! It is not in my Pow'r, I can't be angry with you, I am to be afraid of your Anger, not you of mine; I must not be angry with you, whatever you do.

LUCY
What must not you be angry, let me do what I will?

BLISTER
No, my Dear.

LUCY
Why then, by Goles! I will tell you—I hate you, and I can't abide you.

BLISTER

What have I done to deserve your Hate?

LUCY

You have done nothing; but you are such a great ugly thing, I can't bear to look at you; and if my Papa was to lock me up for a Twelve-month, I shou'd hate you still.

BLISTER

Did you not tell me just now, you wou'd make me your Husband?

LUCY

Yes, so I will for all that.

AIR IV

Now ponder well &c.
Ah be not angry, good dear Sir,
Nor do not tell Papa;
For tho' I can't abide you, Sir,
I'll marry you—O la.—

BLISTER

Well, my Dear, if you can't abide me, I can't help that, nor you can't help it; and if you will not tell your Father, I assure you I will not; besides my Dear, as for liking me, do not give your self any trouble about that, it is the very best reason for marrying me; no Lady now marries any one but whom she hates, hating one another is the chief end of Matrimony. It is what most Couples do before they are Marry'd, and all after it. I fancy you have not a right Notion of a marry'd Life. I suppose you imagine we are to be fond, and kiss, and hug one another as long as we live.

LUCY

Why, an't we?

BLISTER

Ha, ha, ha! an't we! no! How Ignorant it is!
[Aside]
Marrying is nothing but living in the same House together, and going by the same Name; while I am following my Business, you will be following your Pleasure; so that we shall rarely meet but at Meals, and then we are to sit at opposite ends of the Table, and make Faces at each other.

LUCY

I shall like that prodigiously—ah, but there is one thing tho'—an't we to lie together?

BLISTER

A Fortnight, no longer.

LUCY

A Fortnight! that's a long time: but it will be over.

BLISTER
Ay, and then you may have any one else.

LUCY
May I? then I'll have Mr. Thomas, by Goles! why this is pure, la! they told me other Stories. I thought when I had been marry'd, I must have never liked any one but my Husband, and that if I shou'd, he wou'd kill me; bu I thought one thing tho' with my self, that I cou'd like another Man without letting him know it, and then a fig for him.

BLISTER
Ay, ay, they tell Children strange Stories; I warrant they have told you, you must be govern'd by your Husband.

LUCY
My Papa tells me so.

BLISTER
But all the married Women in England will tell you another Story.

LUCY
So they have already, for they say I must not be govern'd by a Husband, and they say another thing too, that you will tell me one Story before Marriage, and another afterwards, for that Marriage alters a Man prodigiously.

BLISTER
No, Child, I shall be just the same Creature I am now, unless in one Circumstance; I shall have a huge pair of Horns upon my Head.

LUCY
Shall you! that's pure, ha, ha, what a Comical figure you will make! but how will you make 'em grow?

BLISTER
It is you that will make 'em grow.

LUCY
Shall I? By Goles! then I'll do't as soon as ever I can; for I long to see 'em! do tell me how I shall do it.

BLISTER
Ev'ry other Man you kiss, I shall have a pair of Horns grow.

LUCY
By Goles, then, you shall have Horns enough; but I fancy you are Jeering me.

AIR V
Buff-Coat.

Ah Sir! I guess
You are a fibbing Creature.

BLISTER
Because, dear Miss,
You know not human Nature.

LUCY
Marry'd Men, I'll be sworn,
I have seen without Horn,

BLISTER
Ah Child! you want art to unlock it:
The Secret here lies,
Men now are so wise,
To carry their Horns in their Pocket.

LUCY
But you shall wear yours on your Head, for I shall like 'em better than any other thing about you.

BLISTER
This Girl's Ignorance will make it easy to discover her; and if I can recover a good round Sum of her Gallant, I shall not be uneasy under my Cuckoldom.

AIR VI
Bartholomew Fair.

The Jokers have said, that Men of my Trade
Sell Drugs so dear.
That by their Bills five hundred per Cent
They often clear:
But when the Gallant, takes what I don't want,
And pays for his Pains,
I'm sure ev'ry Man must own, that it's all clear Gains.
But when, &c.
Well then, Miss, I may depend upon you.

LUCY
And may I depend upon you?

BLISTER
Yes, my Dear.

LUCY
Ah, but don't call me so; I hate you should call me so.

BLISTER
Oh Child, all marry'd People call one another, my Dear, let 'em hate one another as much as they will.

LUCY

Do they? well then my Dear—hum, I think there is not any great matter in the Word neither.

BLISTER
Why, amongst your fine Gentry, there is scarce any meaning in any thing they say.

AIR VII
When our Wives deny
With all reason to Comply,
'Tis still with I can't, my dearest.
When, to seek another Mate,
We leave a Wife we hate,
'Tis still good-by my fairest.
The Courtier who intends
Ne'er to be among your Friends,

Cries, I'll serve you, honest Adam;
When we find our Wives are Whores,
Still we turn 'em out o'Doors,
With your humble Servant Madam.
Well, I'll go to your Papa, and tell him we have agreed upon Matters, and have the Wedding instantly.

LUCY
The sooner the better.

BLISTER
Your Servant, my pretty Dear.

[Exit.

LUCY
Your Servant, my Dear. Nasty, greasy, ugly Fellow. Well, Marriage is a Charming thing tho', I long to be marry'd more than ever I did for any thing in my life; since I am to govern, I'll warrant I'll do it purely. By Goles, I'll make him know who is at Home—let me see, I'll practise a little. Suppose that Chair was my Husband; and ecod by all I can find, a Chair is as proper for a Husband as any thing else; now says my Husband to me, how do you do, my Dear? Lard I my Dear, I don't know how I I do! not the better for you; pray, my Dear, let us Dine early to day. Indeed, my Dear, I can't—do you intend to go abroad to day! No, my Dear: then you will stay at home; no my Dear; shall we ride out? No, my Dear! shall we go a Visiting? No, my Dear.—I will never do any thing I am bid, that I am resolv'd; and then Mr. Thomas, oh good! I am out of my Wits.

AIR VIII
Bessy Bell.

Lo, what swinging Lyes some People will tell!
I thought when another I'd wedded,
I must have bid poor Mr. Thomas farewell,
And none but my Husband have bedded.
But I find I'm deceiv'd, for as Michaelmas Day

Is still the fore-runner of Lammas,
So Wedding another is but the right way
To come at my dear Mr. Thomas.

[Enter **COUPEE**.

Heyday! What fine Gentleman is this?

COUPEE
Cousin, your most obedient, and devoted humble Servant.

LUCY
I find this is one of your fine Gentry, by his not having any meaning in his Words.

COUPEE
I have not the Honour to be known to you, Cousin; but your Father has been so kind to give me Admission to your fair Hands.

LUCY
G-Gemini Cancer! what a fine Charming Man this is!

COUPEE
My Name, Madam, is Coupee, and I have the Honour to be a Dancing-Master.

LUCY
And are you come to teach me to Dance?

COUPEE
Yes, my Dear, I am come to teach you a very pretty Dance, did you never learn to Dance?

LUCY
No Sir, not I, only Mr. Thomas taught me, one, two, three.

COUPEE
That is a very great Fault in your Education, and it will be a great Happiness for you to amend it, by having a Dancing-Master for your Husband.

LUCY
Yes Sir, but I am not to have a Dancing-Master; my Papa says, I am to have a nasty stinking Apothecary.

COUPEE
Your Papa says! what signifies what your Papa says?

LUCY
What must I not mind what my Papa says?

COUPEE
No, no, you are to follow your own Inclinations—I think if she has any Eyes, I may venture to trust

'em—your Father is a very Comical, queer old Fellow, a very odd kind of a silly Fellow, and you ought to laugh at him. I ask Pardon tho' for my Freedom.

LUCY
You need not ask my Pardon, for I am not at all angry, for between you and I, I think him as odd, queer a Fellow, as you can do for your life. I hope you won't tell him what I say.

COUPEE
I tell him! I hate him for his barbarous Usage of you, to lock up a young Lady of Beauty, Wit and Spirit, without ever suffering her to learn to Dance? why Madam, not learning to Dance, is absolute ruin to a young Lady. I suppose he took care enough you shou'd learn to read.

LUCY
Yes, I can read very well.

COUPEE
Ay, there it is; all Parents take care to instruct their Children in low mechanical things, while the genteel Sciences are neglected. Forgive me, Madam, at least, if I throw my self at your Feet, and vow never to rise till lifted up with the elevating fire of your Smiles.

LUCY [Aside]
Lard Sir, I don't know what to say to these fine things—he's a pure Man.

COUPEE
Might I hope to obtain the least spark of your Love, the least spark, Madam, wou'd blow up a Flame in me, that nothing ever cou'd quench. O hide those lovely Eyes, nor dart their fiery Rays upon me, lest I am consumed—shall I hope you will think of me.

LUCY [Aside]
I shall think of you more than I will let you know.

COUPEE
Will you not answer me?

LUCY
La! You make me Blush so, I know not what to say.

COUPEE
Ay, that is from not having learnt to Dance, a Dancing-Master wou'd have cur'd her of that. Let me teach you what to say, that I may hope you will condescend to make me your Husband.

LUCY
No, I won't say that, but—

AIR IX
Tweed Side.

O press me not, Sir, to be Wife

To a Man whom I never can hate;
So sweet a fine Gentleman's Life,
Shou'd never be sour'd with that Fate.
But soon as I marry'd have been,
Ungrateful I will not be nam'd;
Oh stay but a Fortnight, and then,
And then you shall—Oh, I'm asham'd.

COUPEE

A Fortnight! bid me live to the Age of—of—Mr. What's-his-Name, the oldest Man that ever liv'd; live a Fortnight after you are marry'd! No, unless you resolve to have me, I will resolve to put an end to my self.

LUCY

O do not do that, but indeed I never can hate you, and the Apothecary says no Woman marries any Man she does not hate.

COUPEE

Ha, ha, ha! Such mean Fellows as those ev'ry fine Lady must hate; but when they marry fine Gentlemen, they love them as long as they live.

LUCY

O but I wou'd not have you think I love you. I assure you, I don't love you; I have been told I must not tell any Man I love him. I don't love you, indeed I don't.

COUPEE

But may I not hope you will?

LUCY

Lard Sir, I can't help what you hope; it is equal to me what you hope. Miss Jenny says, I must always give my self Airs to a Man I like.

COUPEE

Hope, Madam, at least, you may allow me; the cruellest of your Sex, the greatest Tyrants deny not hope.

LUCY

No, I won't give you the least crumb of hope—hope indeed! what do you take me for? I'll assure you! No, I wou'd not give you the least bit of hope, tho' I was to see you die before my Face. It is a pure thing to give ones self Airs.

COUPEE

Since nothing but my Death will content you, you shall be satisfy'd even at that Price.

[Pulls out his Kitt.

Ha! Cursed Fate? I have no other Instrument of Death about me than a Sword, which won't draw. But I have thought of a way; within the Orchard, there is an Appletree; there, there, Madam! you shall see me hanging by the Neck there.

There shall you see your Dancing-Master die,
As Bateman hang'd for Love—e'en so will I.

LUCY
Oh stay!

AIR X
Lass of Patty's Mill.

When you're like Bateman dead,
Your Ghost will come like him,
And take me out o'bed,
And tear me limb from limb.
If one then of the two
A Ghost or Man's my fate,
I'll go to Bed with you,
E'er out o' Bed with that.

La! Sir, you're so hasty—must I tell you the first time I see you? Miss Jenny Flant-it has been courted these two Years by half a dozen Men, and no body knows which she'll have yet, and must not I be courted at all? I will be courted, indeed so I will.

COUPEE
And so you shall, I will Court you after we are married.

LUCY
But will you indeed?

COUPEE
Yes indeed, but if I shou'd not, there are others enough that wou'd.

LUCY
But I did not think marry'd Women had ever been courted tho'.

COUPEE
That is all owing to your not learning to Dance! why there are abundance of Women who marry for no other reason, as there are several Men who never Court any but marry'd Women.

LUCY
Well then, I don't much care if I do marry you, but hold! There is one thing—but that does not much signify.

COUPEE
What is it, my Dear?

LUCY
Only I promis'd the Apothecary just now; that's all.

COUPEE
Well, shall I fly then, and put ev'ry thing in readiness?

LUCY
Ay do, I'm ready.

COUPEE
One kiss before I go, my dearest Angel, and now one, two, three and away.

[Exit.

LUCY
Oh dear, sweet Man! as handsome as an Angel, and as fine as a Lord. He is handsomer than Mr. Thomas, and Icod! almost as well drest. I see now why my Father wou'd never let me learn to Dance. For, by Goles! if all Dancing-Masters be such fine Men as this, I wonder ev'ry Woman does not Dance away with one. O la, now I think on't, he pull'd out his fidling thing, and I did not ask him to play a Tune upon't—but when we are marry'd, I'll make him play upon't; I'cod, he shall teach me to Dance too—he shall play, and I'll Dance; that will be pure.

AIR XI
Polwarth on the Green.

What Virgin e'er wou'd marry
A nasty Apothecary,
Whose Presence makes
Each thing that she takes
As had as his Physick can be?
Give me the brisk Blade,
Who lives by a Trade,
Abounding with Frolick and Glee;
On his Kit he shall play,
And I'll dance all the Day,
One, two, three; one, two, three.

Hey! what's here? another Lover, I hope; the more the merrier, by Goles!

[Enter **BOOKISH**.

BOOKISH
Unless my Instructions err, you are my Cousin Lucy.

LUCY
So I was christen'd, Sir.

BOOKISH
Why then, most probably you are she.—I suppose it wou'd be needless to inform you of an Affair, wherein you are doubtless already sufficiently instructed by your Parent the Purport of my Arrival here. But as Custom wills, that a Declaration be made on the Male Side, I shall, as briefly as may be, let you

know that my Cousin Goodwill hath signify'd to me his Intentions of a Match between us, which is the Reason that hath drawn me hither from Oxford, and to which, if you comply, I am ready to fulfil his Desire.

LUCY
O la! this Man is worse than the Apothecary; I don't understand one Word in three of what he says.

BOOKISH
Cousin, I attend your Answer.

LUCY
I don't know what to answer you; and while you ask me in such a manner, I won't answer you at all. Why don't you throw your self at my Feet, if you wou'd have me answer you? Other sort of People than you have done it.

BOOKISH
Cousin, you will not, I hope, pretend to inform me what People have done; I know whole Nations have been Idolaters, but I shall not therefore be one. I shall throw my self at no Woman's Feet, for I look on my self as the Superior of the two.

LUCY
What, do you think your self better than me?

BOOKISH
Touching the Sex I do, most certainly.

LUCY
And have you the Impudence to come a courting to me with such a Speech in your Mouth, to me who have just now had a fine Gentleman, a Dancing-Master, Sirrah, at my Feet?

BOOKISH
He occurred to me at my Entrance, giving Offence at once to two of my Senses; my Eyes were wounded by a Coxcomb, and my Nose by a Stink.

LUCY
What, do you call him a Coxcomb? that sweet fine Gentleman, a Coxcomb?

BOOKISH
We have many such sweet Gentlemen at the University, who, it is pity, were not call'd to the same Employment, that they might be of some Use to the Community, for a Beau can be apply'd to no better.

LUCY
By Goles! I thought he was a Beau. Well, Heaven be prais'd, I have liv'd to see a Beau. No Wonder Miss Jenny is so fond of 'em: And I shall have a Beau for a Husband at last, the very thing I always wish'd and long'd for.

AIR XII
Still he's the Man.

I never yet long'd for a thing in my Life,
Not even a Show,
So much as these two Years I've long'd to be Wife
To a dainty fine Beau.
The Ladies of London are sure in the right,
Who are all Day a dressing to get one at Night;
What Woman can ever say, No,
To a dainty fine Beau?

BOOKISH
The properest for you, truly, by what appears.

LUCY
Why you nasty, dirty, ugly, slovenly thing, did you think I'd have you? By Goles! I'd as soon have one of my Father's Carters, ay, or his Cart Horses: Why, you are little better than our Pig-Boy.

BOOKISH
You are not many Degrees from a downright Ideot.

LUCY
Augh! I hate you.

BOOKISH
I cannot say that: But I—vehemently despise you.

AIR XIII
Have you heard of a frolicksome Ditty.

Go marry what Blockhead you will, Miss,
By all that appears I'm afraid,
That terrible Clacker to still, Miss,
A Stick on your Back will be laid. Lucy
Go marry what Woman you may, Sir,
Remember what Lucy has said,
Your Wife, in a Fortnight, will lay, Sir,
A Pair of good Horns on your Head.

BOOKISH
You are, to say the Truth, a very idle, foolish Girl, and I commiserate you.

LUCY
You impudent Fellow! how dare you call me Names? If your Papa suffers you to call me Names, I know those that won't, by Goles! I wish I was a Man, I'd box your Eyes out. You ugly Thing, you! You dirty Thing, you! You nasty, stinking Thing, you!

BOOKISH
A perfect Xantippe!

LUCY

Don't come out with your nasty hard Words here.—I won't speak to you, nor I won't look at you, nor I won't have any thing to do with you.

AIR XIV
We've cheated the Parson.

I wou'd have you to know, you nasty Thing,
That sooner than have you, I'd hear my Knell;
Nay, rather than lead such an Ape in a String,
A Virgin I'd die, and lead Apes in Hell.
Nasty Thing,
Stinking Thing,
I'd die a Maid ere I'd have such a Thing.

BOOKISH

Be not terrify'd, I will not communicate with you any longer.—Truly, I had rather live in the Tub of Diogenes, than with the Wife of Socrates. Mr. Goodwill must be a Block-head, or he wou'd not have sent a Man of Sense to talk with such an Ideot.

[Exit.

LUCY

I am glad he's gone. I had rather have one Beau, than fifty Men of Sense.—I wish my dear Dancing-Master was come back again.—I feel my self I don't know howish.—Lud! I never was so before in my Life!—Heyho!—Lud! I am out of Breath, as if I had run from the bottom of the Stairs to the top, without once stopping.—As sure as can be, I am in Love; ay, that's it; I certainly am in Love.—By Goles! it feels pure tho'.

AIR XV
Ye Nymphs and Silvan Gods.

O all ye Powers above!
I feel my Heart to move,
Pit a pat, pit a pat,
Pit a pat, pit a pat.
O lud! I'm afraid I'm in Love,
Yet I scorn down to lie
Like a Child, and cry:
Since if Miss Jenny's right,
Love's a gentle Dart,
That tickles the Heart,
And tho' it gives us Smart,
Does Joys impart,
Which largely the Pains requite.
O la! what's here? another Beau.

[Enter **QUAVER**.

QUAVER
Madam, your Servant. I suppose my Cousin Goodwill has told you of the Happiness he designs you.

LUCY
No, Sir, my Papa has not told me any thing about you. Who are you, pray?

QUAVER
I have the Honour of being a distant Relation of yours, and I hope to be a nearer one. My Name is Quaver, Madam; I have the Honour to teach some of the first Quality to sing.

LUCY
And are you come to teach me to sing?

QUAVER
I like her Desire to learn to sing, it is a Proof of an excellent Understanding.—Yes; Madam, I will be proud to teach you any thing in my Power; and do believe I shall not yield to any one in the Science of Singing.

LUCY
Well, and I shall be glad to learn; for I have been told, I have a tolerable Voice, only I don't know the Notes.

QUAVER
That, Madam, may be acquired, a Voice can not. A Voice must be the Gift of Nature, and it is the greatest Gift Nature can bestow. All other Perfections, without a Voice, are nothing at all. Musick is allow'd by all wise Men to be the noblest of the Sciences; whoever knows Musick, knows ev'ry thing.

LUCY
Come then, do begin to teach me, for I long to learn.

QUAVER
Hereafter I shall have time enough. But at present I have something of a different Nature to say to you.

LUCY
What have you to say?

AIR XVI
Dimi Caro:

Dearest Charmer!
Will you then bid me tell
What you discern sa well,
By my expiring Sighs,
My doating Eyes,
My doating Eyes?
Look thro' th' instructive Grove,
Each Object prompts to Love;

See how the Turtles play,
Each Object prompts to Love;
All Nature tells you what I'd say.

LUCY
Oh charming! delightful!

QUAVER
May I hope you'll grant—

LUCY
Another Song, and I'll do any thing.

QUAVER
Dearest Creature,
Pride of Nature!
All your Glances
Give me Trances.
Dearest, &c.

LUCY
Oh, I melt, I faint, I swoon, I die!

QUAVER
May I hope you'll be mine?

LUCY
Will you charm me so every Day?

QUAVER
And ev'ry Night too, my Angel.

[Enter **COUPEE**.

COUPEE
Heyday! what do I see? my Mistress in another Man's Arms? Sir, will you do me the Favour to tell me what Business you have with that Lady?

QUAVER
Pray, Sir, be so good as to tell me what Business you have to ask.

COUPEE
Sir!

QUAVER
Sir!

COUPEE

Sir, this Lady is my Mistress.

QUAVER
I beg to be excus'd for that, Sir.

COUPEE
Sir!

QUAVER
Sir!

AIR XVII.
Of all the simple things, &c.

COUPEE
Excuse me, Sir; Zounds, what d'ye mean?
I hope you don't give me the Lye.

QUAVER
Sir, you mistake me quite and clean,
Indeed, good Sir, not I.

COUPEE
Zounds, Sir, if you had, I'ad been mad,
But I'm very glad that you don't.

QUAVER
Do you challenge me, Sir?

COUPEE
Not I, indeed, Sir.

QUAVER
Indeed, Sir, I'm very glad on't.

LUCY
Pray, Gentlemen, what's the Matter? I beseech you speak to me, one of you.

COUPEE
Have I not Reason? Did I not find you in his Arms?

QUAVER
And have I not Reason? Did he not say you was his Mistress, to my Face?

AIR XVIII
Molly Mog.

LUCY

Did Mortal e'er see two such Fools?
For nothing they're going to fight;
I begin to find Men are but Tools,
And both with a Whisper I'll bite.
With you I am ready to go, Sir,
I'll give t'other Fool a Rebuff;
[To **COUPEE**]
Stay you but a Fortnight, or so, Sir,
I warrant I'll grant you enough.
[To **QUAVER**]

QUAVER
Damnation!

COUPEE
Hell and Confusion!

[They draw, **LUCY** runs out.

[Enter **BLISTER**.

BLISTER
For Heaven's sake, Gentlemen! what's the Matter? I profess I am afraid you are both disorder'd. Pray, Sir, give me leave to handle your Pulse; I wish you are not light-headed.

COUPEE
What is it to you, Sir, what I am?

QUAVER
How dare you interfere between Gentlemen, Sirrah?

COUPEE
I have a great Mind to break my Sword about your Head, you Dog.

QUAVER
I have a great Mind to run you thro' the Body, you Rascal.

COUPEE
Do you know who we are?

QUAVER
Ay, ay, do you know whom you have to do with?

BLISTER
Dear Gentlemen, pray Gentlemen.—I wish I had nothing to do with you; I meant no Harm.

COUPEE
So much the worse, Sirrah; so much the worse.

QUAVER

Do you know what it is to anger Gentlemen?

[Enter **GOODWILL**.

GOODWILL

Heyday! what, are you fencing here, Gentlemen?

BLISTER

Fencing, Quotha? they have almost fenced me out of my Senses, I am sure.

COUPEE

I shall take another time.

QUAVER

And so shall I.

GOODWILL

I hope there is no Anger between you. You are nearer Relations than you imagine to each other.—Mr. Quaver, you was sent out of England young; and you, Mr. Coupee, have liv'd all your Life-time in London; but I assure you, you are Cousin-Germans; let me introduce you to each other.

COUPEE

Dear Cousin Quaver.

QUAVER

Dear Cousin Coupee.

BLISTER

It's but a Blow and a Kiss with these Sparks, I find.

COUPEE

I thought there was something about him I cou'd not hurt.

GOODWILL

Here is another Relation too, whom you do not know. This is Mr. Blister, Son to your Uncle Blister the Apothecary.

COUPEE

I hope you will Excuse our Ignorance.

GOODWILL

Yes, Cousin, with all my Heart, since there is no Harm come on't; but if you will take my Advice, you shall both immediately lose some Blood, and I will order each of you a gentle Purge.

[Enter **WORMWOOD**.

WORMWOOD

Your Servant, Cousin Goodwill! How do you do, Master Coupee? How do you do, Master Blister? The Roads are very dirty, but I obey your Summons, you see.

GOODWILL

Mr. Quaver, this is your Cousin Wormwood, the Attorney.

WORMWOOD

I am very glad to see you, Sir. I suppose by so many of our Relations being assembled, this is a Family Law-suit I am come upon. I shall be glad to have my Instructions as soon as possible, for I must carry away some of your Neighbours Goods with Executions, by and by.

GOODWILL

I sent for you on the Account of no Law-Suit this time. In short, I have resolv'd to dispose of my Daughter to one of my Relations, if you like her, Cousin Wormwood, with 10000l, and you shou'd happen to be her Choice—

BLISTER

That's impossible, for she has promis'd me already.

COUPEE

And me.

QUAVER

And me.

WORMWOOD

How! has she promis'd three of you? why then, the two that miss her, will have very good Actions against him that has her.

GOODWILL

Her own Choice must determine; and if that fall on you, Mr. Blister, I must insist on your leaving off your Trade, and living here with me.

BLISTER

No, Sir, I cannot consent to leave off my Trade.

GOODWILL

Pray, Gentlemen, is not the Request reasonable?

ALL

Oh, certainly, certainly.

COUPEE

Ten thousand Pounds to an Apothecary, indeed!

QUAVER

Not leave off his Trade?

COUPEE

If I had been an Apothecary, I believe I shou'd not have made many Words.

GOODWILL

I dare swear you will not, Cousin, if she shou'd make choice of you.

COUPEE

There is some Difference tho' between us; mine is a genteel Profession, and I shall not leave it off on any Account.

GOODWILL

I'll be judg'd by Mr. Quaver here, who has been abroad and seen the World.

QUAVER

Very reasonable, very reasonable.—This Man, I see, has excellent Sense, and can distinguish between Arts and Sciences.

GOODWILL

I am confident it wou'd not be easy to prevail on you to continue the ridiculous Art of teaching People to sing.

QUAVER

Ridiculous Art of teaching to Sing! Do you call Musick an Art, which is the noblest of all Sciences? I thought you a Man of Sense, but I find—

COUPEE

And I find too.

BLISTER

And so do I.

WORMWOOD

Well, it is surprising that Men shou'd be such Fools, that they shou'd hesitate at leaving off their Professions for 10000l.

GOODWILL

Cousin Wormwood, you will leave off your Practice, I am sure.

WORMWOOD

Indeed, Sir, but I will not. I hope you don't put me upon a Footing with Fidlers and Dancing-Masters. No Man need be asham'd of marrying his Daughter to a Practitioner of the Law. What wou'd you do without Lawyers? Who'd know his own Property?

BLISTER

Or without Physicians, who'd know when he was well?

COUPEE

If it was not for Dancing-Masters, Men might as well walk upon their Heads as their Heels.

QUAVER
And if it was not for Singing-Masters, they might as well have been all born dumb.

[Enter **BOOKISH**.

GOODWILL
Heav'n be prais'd, here comes a Man of Sense, who will, I warrant, quit his Fellowship at the first Word, for my Daughter.—Cousin Bookish, I am glad you are come, you have seen my Daughter, I hope.

BOOKISH
Yes, I have seen her, and without Flattery, a most contemptible Creature she is.

ALL
Ha, ha, ha!

GOODWILL
How! how!

BOOKISH
I can scarce allow her the Appellation of Animal rationale. She agrees well with Aristole's Definition of Animal inplume bipes. In fine, such an Animal never occurr'd to me before.

GOODWILL
You are all a Set of intolerable Coxcombs, and I will give my Daughter to none of you.

BLISTER
I shall have her, I believe, without your Consent.

QUAVER
I shall whistle her away without your Leave.

COUPEE
How little he guesses that I shall dance off with her within this Half-hour!

GOODWILL
Ha! Confusion! what do I see! my Daughter in the Hands of that Fellow!

[Enter **LUCY** and **MR THOMAS**.

LUCY
Pray, Papa, give me your Blessing. I hope you won't be angry with me, but I am marry'd to Mr. Thomas.

MR THOMAS
I am afraid the Cloth I wear will be no Recommendation to me; but you may take off that Scandal. I assure you, my Family, which I will not now disown, intitled me to a better Station of Life, nor has my Education been as mean as my present Condition.

GOODWILL

Oh Lucy, Lucy! is this the Return you make to my Fatherly Fondness?

LUCY

Dear Papa, forgive me, I won't do so any more.—Indeed I should have been perjured, if I had not had him.—And I had not had him neither, but that he met me when I was frighten'd, and did not know what I did.

GOODWILL

To marry a Footman?

MR THOMAS

Why look ye, Sir, I am a Footman, 'tis true, but I have good Acquaintance in Life. I have kept very good Company at the Hazard-Table; and when I have other Cloaths on and Money in my Pocket, the Quality will be very glad to see me again.

WORMWOOD

Hark ye, Mr. Goodwill, your Daughter is an Heiress. I'll put you in a way to prosecute this Fellow.

BLISTER

Did you not promise me, Madam?

COUPEE

Ay, did you not promise me, Madam?

QUAVER

And me too?

LUCY

You have none of you any Reason to Complain; if I did promise you all, I promis'd him first.

WORMWOOD

Look ye, Gentlemen, if any of you will employ me, I'll undertake we shall recover part of her Fortune.

BOOKISH

I think the Woman has chose the properest Husband for her, for I confide she can't read.

QUAVER

If you had giv'n your Daughter a good Education, and let her learnt Musick, it wou'd have put softer things into her Head.

BLISTER

This comes of your Contempt of Physick. If she had been kept in a Diet, with a little gentle Bleeding, and Purging, and Vomiting, and Blistering, this had never happen'd.

WORMWOOD

You shou'd have sent her to Town a Term or two, and taken Lodgings for her near the Temple, that she might have conversed with the young Gentlemen of the Law, and seen the World.

AIR XIX
Bush of Boon.

LUCY
Oh dear Papa! don't look so grum;
Forgive me and be good:
For tho' he's not so great as some,
He still is Flesh and Blood.
What tho' he's not so fine as Beaus,
In Gold and Silver gay;
Yet he, perhaps, without their Cloaths,
May have more Charms than they.

MR THOMAS
Your Daughter has marry'd a Man of some Learning, and one who has seen a little of the World, and who by his Love to her, and Obedience to you, will try to deserve your Favours. As for my having worn a Livery, let not that grieve you; as I have liv'd in a great Family, I have seen that no one is respected for what he is, but for what he has; the World pays no regard at present to any thing but Money, and if my own Industry shou'd add to your Fortune, so as to entitle any of my Posterity to Grandeur, it will be no reason against making my Son or Grandson a Lord, that his Father or Grandfather was a Footman.

GOODWILL
Ha! Thou talk'st like a pretty sensible Fellow, and I don't know whether my Daughter has not made a better choice, than she cou'd have done among her Booby Relations. I shall suspend my Judgment at present, and pass it hereafter; according to your behaviour.

MR THOMAS
I will try to deserve it shou'd be in my Favour.

WORMWOOD
I hope, Cousin, you don't expect I shou'd lose my time. I expect Six and Eight Pence for my Journey.

GOODWILL
Thy Profession, I see, has made a Knave of whom Nature meant a Fool. Well, henceforth I am resolv'd to indulge my self in all innocent and moderate Satisfactions, and laugh at my former Folly, and that of others, who think when they have rais'd a Fortune, they shall have any Happiness in bestowing it; since their finding one worthy to inherit it, is a greater Accident, and a greater Blessing, than the Fortune it self. What a Comfort must it be to a Man to think, while he is amassing Riches, that the Reward of all his Labour and Care, and Self-denial will be.
To go a toilsome Journey to the Grave,
And leave his Treasures to a Fool or Knave.

SONG.
Tune, The Yorkshire Ballad.

BLISTER
Had your Daughter been physick'd well, Sir, as she ought,
With Bleeding, and Blist'ring, and Vomit, and Draught,
This Footman had never been once in her Thought,
With his Down, down, &c.

COUPEE
Had pretty Miss been at a Dancing-School bred,
Had her Feet but been taught the right Manner to tread,
Gad's Curse! 'twould have put better things in her Head,
Than his Down, down, &c.

QUAVER
Had she learnt, like fine Ladies, instead of her Prayers,
To languish and die at Italian soft Airs.
A Footman had never thus tickled her Ears,
With his Down, down, &c.

LUCY
You may Physick, and Musick, and Dancing enhance,
In One I have got them all three by good Chance,
My Doctor he'll be, and he'll teach me to dance,
With his Down, down, &c.
And though soft Italians the Ladies controul,
He swears he can charm a fine Lady, by Gole!
More than an Italian can do for his Soul,
With a Down, down, &c.
My Fate then, Spectators, hangs on your Decree,
I have brought kind Papa here, at last, to agree;
If you'll pardon the Poet, he will pardon me,
With my Down, down, &c.
Let not a poor Farce then nice Criticks pursue,
But like honest-hearted good-natur'd Men do,
And clap to please us, who have sweat to please you,
With our Down, down, &c.

CHORUS
Let not a poor Farce then, &c.

Henry Fielding – A Short Biography

Henry Fielding was born at Sharpham Park, near Glastonbury, in Somerset on April 22nd 1707. His early years were spent on his parents' farm in Dorset. His family were well to do. His father was a colonel, later a general in the army, his maternal grandfather was a judge of the Queen's Bench and his second cousin would later become the fourth Earl of Denbigh.

He was educated at Eton where he became lifelong friends with William Pitt the Elder.

An early romance ended disastrously and with it his removal to London and the beginnings of a glittering literary career. Early advice on this came from another cousin, the noted poet, Lady Mary Wortley Montagu. Fielding published his first play, at age 21, in 1728.

Later that same year he journeyed to the University at Leiden, the oldest University in Holland, to study classics and law. However, within months, with funds low, mainly due to his father cutting off his allowance, he was forced to return to London and to write for the theatre.

It was a twist of fate that was to ensure him both notoriety and a reputation that would exceed his wildest expectations.

He was prolific, sometimes writing six plays a year, but he did like to poke fun at the authorities. His plays were thought to be the final straw for the authorities in their attempts to bring some sense of order to an increasingly provocative Theatre. Some of the plays denigrated, insulted, or criticised either the King, or his Government, in ways that caused them to react with their preferred response; a new law. Although the Golden Rump was cited as the play on which the authorities based their need for better regulation it is thought that the constant stepping over the line by Fielding in his own works was the actual trigger for, and target of, the new law. No copy of the play, The Golden Rump, exists today and it seems never, in fact, to have been performed or perhaps even published. Various accounts attribute Fielding as the author and others say it was secretly commissioned by Walpole himself to bring about the conditions necessary to bring the Act before Parliament.

Whatever the validity in 1737 The Theatrical Licensing Act was passed. At a stroke political satire was almost impossible. Fielding much admired – and reviled – for his savaging of Sir Robert Walpole government was rendered mute. Any playwright who was viewed with suspicion by the Government now found an audience difficult to find and therefore Theatre owners now toed the Government line, works only being available for performance after review by the Lord Chamberlain. A process that was to last in England, although greatly amended in 1843, until 1968.

Fielding was practical in the circumstances and ironically stopped writing to once again take up his career in the practice of law. He became a barrister after studying at Middle Temple – he completed the six year course in only three. By this time he had also married Charlotte Craddock, his first wife, and they would go on to have five children, but only a daughter would survive. Charlotte died in 1744 but was immortalised as the heroine in both Tom Jones and Amelia.

As a businessman Fielding lacked any financial education and he and his family often endured bouts of poverty. He did however find a wealthy benefactor in the shape of Ralph Allen, who was to later feature in the novel Tom Jones as the character foundation for Squire Allworthy.

Fielding never stopped writing political satire or satires of current arts and letters. The Tragedy of Tragedies, for which Hogarth designed the frontispiece, had, for example, some success as a printed play. He also contributed a number of works to journals of the day as well as writing for Tory periodicals, usually under the name of "Captain Hercules Vinegar". His choice of name reveals his style. But then again his other later nom de plumes are also revealing; Sir Alexander Drawcansir and Scriblerus Secundus

In 1731 Fielding wrote "The Roast Beef of Old England", which is used by the Royal Navy and the United States Marine Corps. It was later arranged by Richard Leveridge.

During the late 1730s and early 1740s Fielding continued to air his liberal and anti-Jacobite views in satirical articles and newspapers. He was nothing if not passionate and this adherence to principles would eventually have great reward for him.

Fielding was much put out by the success of Samuel Richardson's Pamela, or Virtue Rewarded. His reaction was to spur him into writing a novel. In 1741 this first novel, Shamela, was a success, an anonymous parody of Richardson's melodramatic novel. It is a satire that follows the model of the famous Tory satirists of the previous generation; Swift and Gay.

On the tail of this success came Joseph Andrews in 1742. Begun as a parody on Pamela's brother, Joseph, it swiftly developed and matured into an accomplished novel in its own right and marked the entrance of Fielding as a major English novelist.

In 1743, he published a novel in the Miscellanies volume III (which was, in fact, the first volume of the Miscellanies). This was The History of the Life of the Late Mr Jonathan Wild the Great. Sometimes this is cited as his first novel, as he did indeed begin writing it before Shamela, but it is now placed later. Once again Fielding returns to satire and one of his favourite subjects – Sir Robert Walpole. In it he draws a parallel between Walpole and Jonathan Wild, the infamous gang leader and highwayman. He implicitly compares the Whig party in Parliament to a gang of thieves, whose leader, Walpole, lives only for his desire and ambition to be a "Great Man" (a common epithet for Walpole) and should culminate only in the antithesis of greatness: being hung from a gallows. By now Walpole had resigned as Prime minster after some 20 years. Fielding could now re-affirm political allegiance back to the Whigs and would now denounce both Tories and Jacobites in his writings.

Although Fielding was never afraid to court controversy he published his next work anonymously in 1746, and perhaps with good reason. The Female Husband, a fictionalized account of a sensational case of a female transvestite who was tried for duping another woman into marriage. This was one of a number of small published pamphlets at sixpence a time. Though a minor item in both length and his canon it shows Fielding's consistent interest and examination of fraud, sham, and masks but, of course, his subject matter was rather sensational.

In 1747, three years after Charlotte's death and ignoring public opinion, he married her former maid, Mary Daniel, who was pregnant. Mary bore him five children altogether; three daughters, who died early and sons William and Allen.

Undoubtedly the masterpiece of Fielding's career was the novel Tom Jones, published in 1749. It is a wonderfully and carefully constructed picaresque novel following the convoluted and hilarious tale of how a foundling came into a fortune.

Fielding was a consistent anti-Jacobite and a keen supporter of the Church of England. This led to him now being richly rewarded with the position of London's Chief Magistrate. The position itself had no salary attached but he refused all manner of bribes during his tenure, which was most unusual. Fielding continued to write and his career both literary and professional continued to climb.

In 1749 he joined with his younger half-brother John, to help found what was the nascent forerunner to a London police force, the Bow Street Runners. (He and his siblings were quite some partnership. His younger sister, Sarah, also became a well known novelist)

His influence here was undoubted. He and John did much to help the cause of judicial reform and to help improve prison conditions. His pamphlets and enquiries included a proposal for the abolition of public hangings. This was not, as you would think because he was opposed to capital punishment as such—indeed, for example, in his 1751 presiding over the trial of the notorious criminal James Field, he found him guilty in a robbery and sentenced him to hang.

In January 1752 Fielding started a fortnightly periodical titled The Covent-Garden Journal, which he would publish under the colourful pseudonym of "Sir Alexander Drawcansir, Knt. Censor of Great Britain" until November of the same year. In this periodical, Fielding directly challenged the "armies of Grub Street" and the other periodical writers of the day in a conflict that would eventually become the Paper War of 1752–3.

Fielding then published, in 1753, "Examples of the interposition of Providence in the Detection and Punishment of Murder, a work in which, rejecting the deistic and materialistic visions of the world, he wrote in favour of the belief in God's presence and divine judgement, arguing that the rise of murder rates was due to neglect of the Christian religion. In 1753 he would add to this with Proposals for making an effectual Provision for the Poor.

Fielding's ardent commitment to the cause of justice as a great humanitarian in the 1750s unfortunately coincided with a rapid deterioration in his health. Such was his decline that in the summer of 1754 he travelled, with Mary and his daughter, to Portugal in search of a cure. Gout, asthma, dropsy and other afflictions forced him to use crutches. His health continued to fail alarmingly.

Henry Fielding died in Lisbon two months later on October 8th, 1754.

His tomb is in the city's English Cemetery (Cemitério Inglês), which is now the graveyard of St. George's Church, Lisbon.

Henry Fielding – A Concise Bibliography

The Masquerade, a poem
Love in Several Masques, a play, 1728
Rape Upon Rape, a play, 1730.
The Temple Beau, a play, 1730
The Author's Farce, a play, 1730
The Letter Writers, a play, 1731
The Tragedy of Tragedies; or, The Life and Death of Tom Thumb the Great, a play, 1731
Grub-Street Opera, a play, 1731
The Roast Beef of Old England, 1731
The Modern Husband, a play, 1732
The Mock Doctor, a play, 1732
The Lottery, a play, 1732

The Covent Garden Tragedy, a play, 1732
The Miser, a play, 1732
The Old Debauchees, a play 1732
The Intriguing Chambermaid, a play, 1734
Don Quixote in England, a play, 1734
Pasquin, a play, 1736
Eurydice Hiss'd, a play, 1737
The Historical Register for the Year 1736, a play, 1737
An Apology for the Life of Mrs. Shamela Andrews, a novel, 1741
The History of the Adventures of Joseph Andrews & his Friend, Mr. Abraham Abrams, a novel, 1742
The Life and Death of Jonathan Wild, the Great, a novel, 1743.
Miscellanies – collection of works, 1743, contained the poem Part of Juvenal's Sixth Satire, Modernized in Burlesque Verse
The Female Husband or the Surprising History of Mrs Mary alias Mr George Hamilton, who was convicted of having married a young woman of Wells and lived with her as her husband, taken from her own mouth since her confinement, a pamphlet, fictionalized report, 1746
The History of Tom Jones, a Foundling, a novel, 1749
A Journey from this World to the Next – 1749
Amelia, a novel, 1751
"Examples of the interposition of Providence in the Detection and Punishment of Murder containing above thirty cases in which this dreadful crime has been brought to light in the most extraordinary and miraculous manner; collected from various authors, ancient and modern", 1752
The Covent Garden Journal, a periodical, 1752
Journal of a Voyage to Lisbon, a travel narrative, 1755
The Fathers: Or, the Good-Natur'd Man, a play, published posthumously in 1778

Other Works (Undated)
An Old Man or The Virgin Unmasked
Miss Lucy in Town, a Play, a sequel to The Virgin Unmasked
Plutus with William Young from the Greek play by Aristophanes.
The Temple Beau, a play
The Wedding Beau, a play
The Welsh Opera
Tumble-Down Dick
An Essay on Conversation, an Essay
The True Patriot, a letter

www.ingramcontent.com/pod-product-compliance
Lightning Source LLC
Chambersburg PA
CBHW021948040426
42448CB00008B/1292